Math Around Us

Shapes in the Kitchen

Tracey Steffora

Heinemann Library
Chicago, Illinois

www.heinemannraintree.com
Visit our website to find out more information about Heinemann-Raintree books.

To order:
☎ Phone 888-454-2279
💻 Visit www.heinemannraintree.com to browse our catalog and order online.

© 2011 Heinemann Library
an imprint of Capstone Global Library, LLC
Chicago, Illinois

Edited by Rebecca Rissman, Tracey Steffora, and Catherine Veitch
Designed by Joanna Hinton-Malivoire
Picture research by Elizabeth Alexander
Production by Victoria Fitzgerald
Originated by Capstone Global Library Ltd
Printed and bound in the United States of America,
North Mankato, MN

14 13 12 11 10
10 9 8 7 6 5 4 3 2 1

Library of Congress Cataloging-in-Publication Data
Steffora, Tracey.
  Shapes in the kitchen / Tracey Steffora.
    p. cm.—(Math around us)
  Includes bibliographical references and index.
  ISBN 978-1-4329-4922-8 (hc)—ISBN 978-1-4329-4930-3 (pb) 1. Shapes—Juvenile literature. 2. Geometry—Juvenile literature. I. Title.
  QA445.5.S735 2011
  516'.15—dc22
                              2010032456

Acknowledgments
The author and publisher are grateful to the following for permission to reproduce photographs: Alamy pp. 7 (© Clearviewstock), 11 (© Palabra), 22 (© Directphoto.org), 23 glossary – tile (© Clearviewstock); GAP Interiors p. 5 (Spike Powell); Getty Images pp. 4 (Travel Ink/Gallo Images), 12 (B. Sporrer/ J.Skowronek/ StockFood Creative); iStockphoto p. 20 (© Ljiljana Pavkov); Photolibrary p. 19 (Lynx/Iconotec.com); Shutterstock pp. 8 (© Michael C. Gray), 9 (© David Hughes), 13 (© oku), 15 (© AnnaIA), 16 (© Argunova), 17 (© VolkOFF-ZS-BP), 20 background (© Blackbirds), 21 (© highviews), 23 glossary - cutting board (© VolkOFF-ZS-BP), 23 glossary – samosa (© highviews).

Cover photograph of a meal viewed from above reproduced with permission of Getty Images (Andy Crawford/Dorling Kindersley), wood pattern reproduced with permission of Shutterstock (© Blackbirds). Back cover photograph of a napkin reproduced with permission of iStockphoto (© Ljiljana Pavkov), wood pattern reproduced with permission of Shutterstock (© Blackbirds).

We would like to thank Nancy Harris, Dee Reid, and Diana Bentley for their assistance in the preparation of this book.

Every effort has been made to contact copyright holders of material reproduced in this book. Any omissions will be rectified in subsequent printings if notice is given to the publisher.

Contents

Shapes Around Us

Shapes are everywhere.

There are many shapes in the
kitchen.

Squares

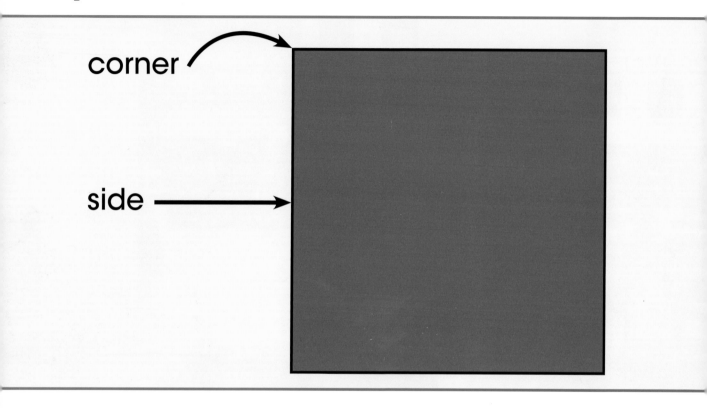

A square has four sides.

A square has four corners.

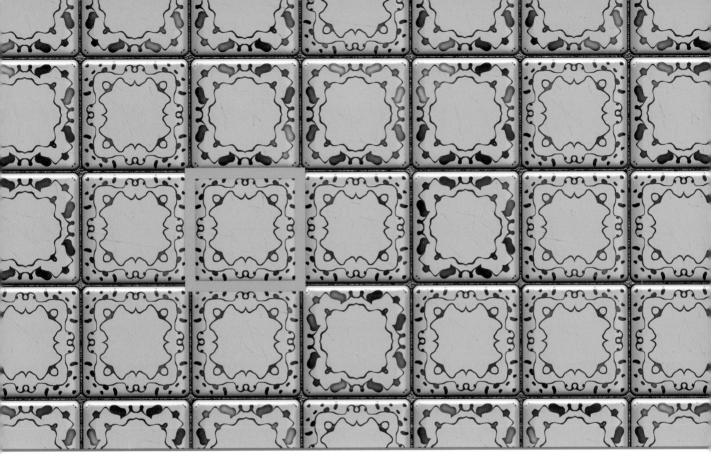

This tile is a square.

This cheese is a square.

This window is a square.

Circles

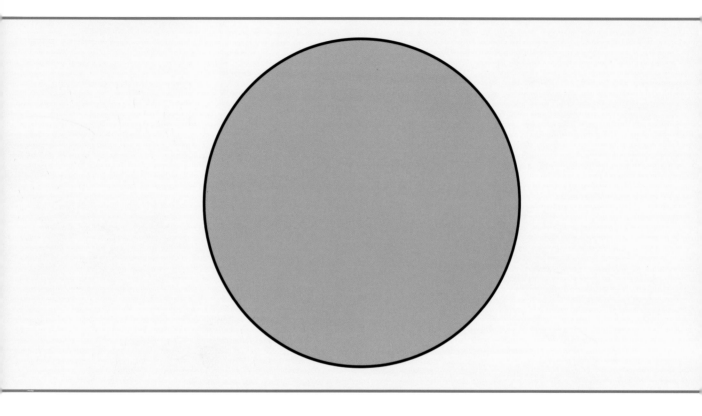

A circle is a round shape.

It has no corners.

This drain is a circle.

This apple is a circle.

This plate is a circle.

Rectangles

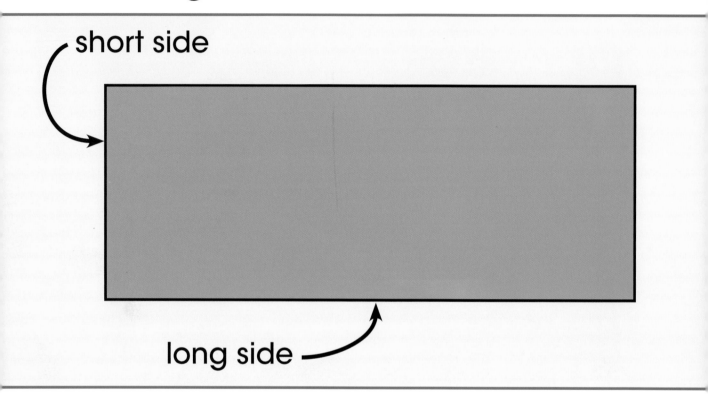

A rectangle has four sides.

A rectangle has four corners.

This door is a rectangle.

This sponge is a rectangle.

This cutting board is a rectangle.

Triangles

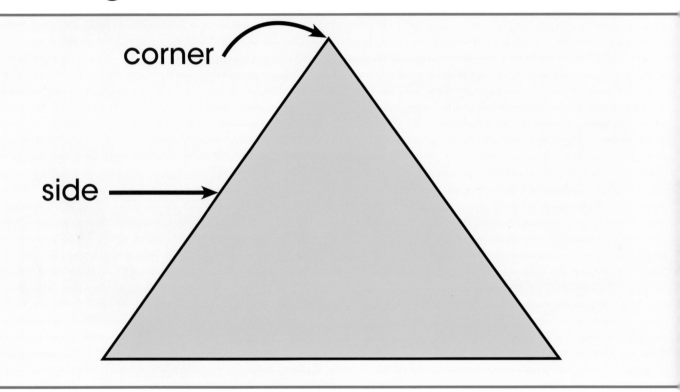

A triangle has three sides.

A triangle has three corners.

This sandwich is a triangle.

This napkin is a triangle.

This samosa is a triangle.

Shapes in the Kitchen

How many shapes can you see?

Picture Glossary

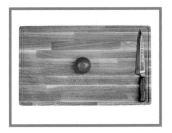 **cutting board** a board used for cutting or chopping food

 **samosa** a triangular food filled with meat or vegetables

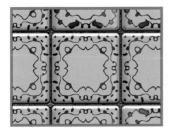 **tile** a piece of material used to cover floors or walls

Index

Notes to Parents and Teachers

Before reading

Review the basic shapes circle, square, rectangle, and triangle with children. Have children name things in their environment that demonstrate each of the shapes. You might also show them that if you cut a potato in half, you will have a curvilinear shape that can be dipped in ink or paint to make a round or oval stamp (depending on which way you slice it).

After reading

• Have childen pay attention to shapes during lunch and report back which shapes they found in their food or food containers.

• Extend by reviewing or introducing children to other shapes, such as oval, ellipse, rhombus, diamond, or hexagon. Discuss the characteristics of these shapes and have children identify them in their environment.